CONTENTS

Introduction

Whether you have decided to avoid meat and fish completely, or simply want to cut down on your intake for a healthier diet, this book will show how exciting vegetarian cookery has become. Gone are the days of heavy, unappetizing dishes; these recipes use a wide variety of fresh, wholesome ingredients to produce meals that are good for your taste buds as well as your health.

When shopping with a truly vegetarian meal in mind, make sure you are not buying animal products unawares. Choose cheese that is made from vegetarian rennet, buy agar-agar or gelozone instead of gelatine and select vegetarian suet instead of beef suet. Stock your store cupboard with a selection of ingredients to keep your diet healthily varied. Flours, grains, pastas and pulses are essential for bulk and as staple ingredients, and a good selection of dried or fresh spices and herbs is always useful. Nuts, seeds and dried fruits are a good source of proteins, vitamins and minerals.

A staple base for many vegetarian dishes is a good stock. A recipe for a fresh vegetable stock is given on page 34. Make a whole batch of stock at one go; it will keep for up to 3 days in the refrigerator, or for up to 3 months if frozen. Store the stock in small containers so that you can defrost just the amount you need for a recipe. Salt is not added when cooking the stock; it is better to season it according to the dish in which it is to be used.

More and more people prefer vegetarian food these days, and this book provides a wide range of dishes to try. Even meat eaters will be satisfied, thanks to the imagination that has gone into devising each recipe, and the wide range of flavours and ingredients used. Baked Aubergine, Basil & Mozzarella Rolls, Tagliatelle with Broccoli & Blue Cheese Sauce, Fiery Salsa with Tortilla Chips, Mexican Chilli Corn Pie – these are just a few of the delicious recipes to be found in this inspiring book.

WHAT'S COOKING?

VEGETARIAN

First published in Great Britain in 1997 by
Parragon
Unit 13–17
Avonbridge Trading Estate
Atlantic Road
Avonmouth
Bristol BS11 9QD

ISBN: 0-7525-2254-X

Produced by Haldane Mason, London

Acknowledgements
Art Director: Ron Samuels
Editors: Jo-Anne Cox, Charles Dixon-Spain
Design: Zoë Mellors
Photography: Sue Atkinson, Iain Bagwell, Joff Lee,
Patrick McLeavey

Printed in Italy

Material in this book has previously appeared in
Vegetarian Chinese Cooking by Wendy Lee, *Vegetarian
Dinner Parties* by Sue Ashworth, *Vegetarian Main
Meals* by Kathryn Hawkins and *Vegetarian Thai
Cooking* by Cara Hobday

Note
Cup measurements in this book are for
American cups. Tablespoons are assumed to be
15 ml. Unless otherwise stated, milk is assumed
to be full fat, eggs are standard size 3 and
pepper is freshly ground black pepper.

Herb, Toasted Nut & Paprika Cheese Nibbles

These tiny cheese balls are rolled in fresh herbs, toasted nuts or paprika to make tasty nibbles for parties, buffets, or pre-dinner drinks.

SERVES 4

125 g/4 oz/³⁄₄ cup Ricotta
125 g/4 oz/1¼ cups Double Gloucester (brick) cheese, grated
2 tsp chopped parsley • pepper
60 g/2 oz/½ cup chopped mixed nuts
3 tbsp chopped fresh herbs, such as parsley, chives, marjoram, lovage and chervil
2 tbsp mild paprika
sprigs of fresh herbs, to garnish

1 Mix together the Ricotta and Double Gloucester (brick) cheeses. Add the parsley and pepper, and mix together until combined.

2 Form the mixture into small balls. Cover and chill for about 20 minutes to firm.

3 Scatter the chopped nuts on to a baking sheet (cookie sheet) and place them under a preheated grill (broiler) until lightly browned. Take care as they can easily burn. Leave them to cool.

4 Sprinkle the nuts, herbs and paprika into 3 separate small bowls. Divide the cheese balls into 3 equal piles and then roll 1 quantity in the nuts, 1 quantity in the herbs and 1 quantity in the paprika.

5 Arrange on a serving platter. Chill until ready to serve, and then garnish with sprigs of fresh herbs.

Cheese, Garlic & Herb Pâté

This wonderfully soft cheese pâté is fragrant with the aroma of fresh herbs.

SERVES 4

15 g/½ oz/1 tbsp butter • 1 garlic clove, crushed
3 spring onions (scallions), chopped finely
125 g/4 oz/¾ cup full-fat soft cheese
2 tbsp chopped mixed fresh herbs, such as parsley, chives, marjoram, oregano and basil
175 g/6 oz/2¼ cups mature (sharp) Cheddar, grated
pepper
4–6 slices of white bread from a medium-cut sliced loaf
mixed salad leaves (greens) and cherry tomatoes, to serve

To garnish:
ground paprika • sprigs of fresh herbs

1 Melt the butter in a small frying pan (skillet) and gently fry the garlic and spring onions (scallions) for 3–4 minutes, until softened. Allow to cool.

2 Beat the soft cheese in a large mixing bowl, then add the garlic and spring onions (scallions). Stir in the herbs, mixing well. Add the Cheddar and work the mixture together to form a stiff paste. Cover and chill until ready to serve.

3 Toast the slices of bread on both sides, then cut off the crusts. Using a sharp bread knife, cut through the slices horizontally to make very thin slices. Cut into triangles and then lightly grill (broil) the untoasted sides.

4 Arrange the mixed salad leaves (green) on 4 serving plates with the tomatoes. Pile the pâté on top and sprinkle with a little paprika. Garnish with fresh herbs and serve with the Melba toast.

Baked Aubergine (Eggplant), Basil & Mozzarella Rolls

Thin slices of aubergine (eggplant) are fried in olive oil and garlic, then topped with pesto sauce and Mozzarella.

SERVES 4

2 aubergines (eggplant), sliced thinly lengthways
5 tbsp olive oil • 1 garlic clove, crushed
4 tbsp pesto sauce
175 g / 6 oz / 2¼ cups Mozzarella, grated
basil leaves, torn into pieces
salt and pepper
fresh basil leaves, to garnish

1 Sprinkle the aubergine (eggplant) slices liberally with salt and leave for 10–15 minutes to extract the bitter juices. Turn the slices over and repeat. Rinse well with cold water and drain on paper towels.

2 Heat the olive oil in a large frying pan (skillet) and add the garlic. Fry the aubergine (eggplant) slices lightly on both sides, a few at a time. Drain them on paper towels.

3 Spread the pesto on to one side of the aubergine (eggplant) slices. Top with the grated Mozzarella and sprinkle with the torn basil leaves. Season with a little salt and pepper. Roll up the slices and secure with wooden cocktail sticks (toothpicks).

4 Arrange the aubergine (eggplant) rolls in a greased ovenproof baking dish. Place in a preheated oven, 180°C/350°F/Gas Mark 4, and bake for 8–10 minutes.

5 Transfer the rolls to a warmed serving plate. Scatter with fresh basil leaves and serve at once.

Fiery Salsa with Tortilla Chips

Make this Mexican-style salsa to perk up jaded palates. Its lively flavours really get the tastebuds going.

SERVES 6

2 small red chillies
1 tbsp lime or lemon juice
2 large ripe avocados
5 cm/2 inch piece cucumber
2 tomatoes, peeled
1 small garlic clove, crushed
few drops of Tabasco sauce • salt and pepper
lime or lemon slices, to garnish
tortilla chips, to serve

1 Remove and discard the stem and seeds from 1 chilli. Chop very finely and place in a mixing bowl. To make a chilli 'flower' for garnish, slice the remaining chilli from the stem to the tip several times without removing the stem. Place in a bowl of cold water, so that the 'petals' open out.

2 Add the lime or lemon juice to the mixing bowl. Halve, stone (pit) and peel the avocados. Add to the mixing bowl and mash with a fork. (The lime or lemon juice prevents the avocado from turning brown.)

3 Chop the cucumber and tomatoes finely and add to the avocado mixture with the crushed garlic. Season the dip to taste with Tabasco sauce, salt and pepper.

4 Transfer the dip to a serving bowl. Garnish with slices of lime or lemon and the chilli flower. Put the bowl on a large plate, surround with tortilla chips and serve.

Mint & Bean Dip

This dip is ideal for pre-dinner drinks or handing around at a party, accompanied by crisps and colourful vegetable crudités.

SERVES 6

175 g / 6 oz / 1 cup dried cannellini beans
1 small garlic clove, crushed
1 bunch spring onions (scallions), chopped roughly
handful of fresh mint leaves
2 tbsp tahini (sesame seed paste) • 2 tbsp olive oil
1 tsp ground cumin
1 tsp ground coriander • lemon juice
salt and pepper • sprigs of fresh mint, to garnish

To serve:
fresh vegetable crudités, such as cauliflower florets, carrots, cucumber, radishes and (bell) peppers

1 Soak the cannellini beans overnight in plenty of cold water.

2 Rinse and drain the beans, put them into a large saucepan and cover them with cold water. Bring to the boil and boil rapidly for 10 minutes. Reduce the heat, cover and simmer until tender.

3 Drain the beans and transfer them to a bowl or food processor. Add the garlic, spring onions (scallions), mint, tahini and olive oil.

4 Blend the mixture for about 15 seconds, or mash well by hand, until smooth.

5 Transfer the mixture to a bowl and season with cumin, coriander, lemon juice, salt and pepper, according to taste. Mix well, cover and leave in a cool place for 30 minutes to allow the flavours to develop.

6 Spoon the dip into serving bowls, garnish with sprigs of fresh mint and surround with vegetable crudités.

Hot & Sour Soup

A traditional staple of the Thai diet, this delicious and nourishing vegetarian soup is sold on street corners, at food bars and by mobile vendors all over the country.

SERVES 4

1 tbsp sunflower oil
250 g/8 oz smoked tofu (bean curd), sliced
90 g/3 oz/1 cup shiitake mushrooms, sliced
2 tbsp chopped fresh coriander (cilantro)
125 g/4 oz/2 cups watercress
1 red chilli, sliced finely, to garnish

Stock:

1 tbsp tamarind pulp
2 dried red chillies, chopped
2 kaffir lime leaves, torn in half
2.5 cm/1 inch piece ginger root, chopped
5 cm/2 inch piece galangal, chopped
1 stalk lemon grass, chopped
1 onion, quartered
1 litre/1¾ pints/4 cups cold water

1 Put all the ingredients for the stock into a saucepan and bring to the boil. Simmer for 5 minutes. Remove from the heat and strain, reserving the stock.

2 Heat the oil in a wok or large, heavy frying pan (skillet) and cook the tofu (bean curd) over a high heat for about 2 minutes, stirring constantly. Pour in the strained stock.

3 Add the mushrooms and coriander (cilantro), and boil for 3 minutes.

4 Add the watercress and boil for 1 minute more. Serve at once, garnished with chilli slices.

Spinach & Mascarpone Soup

This delicious soup has Mascarpone cheese stirred through it to give it the most wonderful texture and flavour.

SERVES 4

60 g/2 oz/4 tbsp butter
1 bunch spring onions (scallions), trimmed and chopped
2 celery sticks, chopped
350 g/12 oz/3 cups spinach or sorrel, or 3 bunches watercress
900 ml/1½ pints/3½ cups Vegetable Stock (page 34)
250 g/8 oz Mascarpone cheese • 1 tbsp olive oil
2 slices thick-cut bread, cut into cubes
½ tsp caraway seeds • salt and pepper
sesame bread sticks, to serve

1 Melt half the butter in a very large saucepan. Add the spring onions (scallions) and celery, and cook gently for about 5 minutes, until softened. Pack the spinach, sorrel or watercress into the saucepan. Add the stock and bring to the boil; then reduce the heat and simmer, covered, for 15–20 minutes.

2 Transfer the soup to a blender or food processor and blend until smooth, or rub through a sieve. Return the soup to the saucepan. Add the Mascarpone cheese and heat gently, stirring, until smooth and blended. Season to taste.

3 Heat the remaining butter with the oil in a frying pan (skillet). Add the bread cubes and fry in the hot fat until golden brown, adding the caraway seeds towards the end of cooking, so that they do not burn.

4 Ladle the soup into 4 warmed bowls. Sprinkle with the croûtons and serve at once, accompanied by the sesame bread sticks.

Mango Salad

This popular Thai salad is an unusual combination of ingredients, but works well as long as the mango is very unripe. Paw-paw (papaya) can be used instead, if you prefer. The components of the salad can be prepared ahead, but should not be assembled until just before serving, so that the flavours remain distinct.

SERVES 4

1 lollo biondo lettuce, or any crunchy lettuce
15 g/½ oz fresh coriander (cilantro) leaves
1 large unripe mango, peeled and
cut into long thin shreds
1 small red chilli, deseeded and chopped finely
2 shallots, chopped finely
2 tbsp lemon juice
1 tbsp light soy sauce
6 roasted canned chestnuts, quartered

1 Line a serving plate or watermelon basket with the lettuce and coriander (cilantro).

2 Soak the mango briefly in cold water, in order to remove any syrup.

3 Meanwhile, make the dressing. Combine the chilli, shallots, lemon juice and soy sauce in a small bowl.

4 Drain the mango, combine with the chestnuts and spoon on to the lettuce and coriander (cilantro).

5 Pour over the dressing and serve immediately.

Pink Grapefruit, Avocado & Dolcelatte Salad

**Fresh pink grapefruit segments,
ripe avocados and sliced Italian Dolcelatte
cheese make a deliciously different
salad combination.**

SERVES 4

*½ cos (romaine) lettuce
½ oak leaf lettuce
2 pink grapefruit • 2 ripe avocados
175 g/ 6 oz Dolcelatte cheese, sliced thinly
sprigs of fresh basil to garnish*

Dressing:
*4 tbsp olive oil • 1 tbsp white wine vinegar
salt and pepper*

1 Arrange the lettuce leaves on 4 serving plates or in a salad bowl.

2 Remove the peel and pith from the grapefruit with a sharp serrated knife, catching the grapefruit juice in a bowl.

3 Segment the grapefruit by cutting down each side of the membrane. Remove all the membrane. Arrange the segments on the serving plates.

4 Peel, stone (pit) and slice the avocados, dipping them in the grapefruit juice to prevent them from going brown. Arrange the slices on the salad with the Dolcelatte cheese.

5 To make the dressing, combine any remaining grapefruit juice with the olive oil and wine vinegar. Season with salt and pepper, mixing well.

6 Drizzle the dressing over the salads. Garnish with fresh basil leaves and serve at once.

Red Onion, Cherry Tomato & Pasta Salad

Pasta tastes perfect in this lively salad.

SERVES 4

175 g/ 6 oz pasta shapes
1 yellow (bell) pepper, halved, cored and deseeded
2 small courgettes (zucchini), sliced
1 red onion, sliced thinly
125 g/ 4 oz cherry tomatoes, halved
salt • sprigs of fresh basil, to garnish

Dressing:
4 tbsp olive oil • 2 tbsp red wine vinegar
2 tsp lemon juice • 1 tsp Dijon mustard
½ tsp caster (superfine) sugar • salt and pepper
handful of fresh basil leaves, torn into small pieces

1 Cook the pasta in a saucepan of boiling, salted water for about 8 minutes, or until just tender.

2 Meanwhile, place the (bell) pepper halves, skin-side uppermost, under a preheated grill (broiler) until they just begin to char. Leave them to cool, then peel and slice into strips.

3 Cook the courgettes (zucchini) in a small amount of boiling, lightly salted water for 3–4 minutes, until cooked, yet still crunchy. Drain and refresh under cold running water to cool quickly.

4 To make the dressing, mix together the oil, wine vinegar, lemon juice, mustard and sugar. Season well with salt and pepper and add the torn basil leaves.

5 Drain the pasta well and transfer to a large serving bowl. Add the dressing and toss well. Add the (bell) pepper, courgettes (zucchini), onion and cherry tomatoes,

stirring to combine. Cover and leave at room temperature for about 30 minutes to allow the flavours to develop. Serve, garnished with sprigs of fresh basil.

Tagliatelle with Broccoli & Blue Cheese Sauce

This is a delicious combination of tagliatelle with Gorgonzola and Mascarpone cheese sauce.

SERVES 4

300 g/10 oz tagliatelle tricolore (plain, spinach- and tomato-flavoured noodles)
250 g/8 oz broccoli, broken into small florets
350g/12 oz/1½ cups Mascarpone cheese
125 g/4 oz/1 cup Gorgonzola cheese, chopped
1 tbsp chopped fresh oregano • 30 g/1 oz/2 tbsp butter
salt and pepper • sprigs of fresh oregano, to garnish
grated Parmesan cheese, to serve

1 Cook the tagliatelle in a pan of boiling, lightly salted water until just tender, or according to the instructions on the packet. The Italians call this *al dente*, which literally means 'to the tooth'.

2 Meanwhile, cook the broccoli florets in a small amount of lightly salted, boiling water. Avoid overcooking the broccoli, so that it retains its colour and texture.

3 Heat the Mascarpone and Gorgonzola cheeses together gently in a large saucepan until they have melted. Stir in the oregano and season to taste with salt and pepper.

4 Drain the pasta thoroughly. Return to the saucepan and add the butter, tossing the tagliatelle to coat. Drain the broccoli thoroughly and add to the pasta with the sauce, tossing gently to mix.

5 Divide the pasta between 4 warmed serving plates. Garnish with sprigs of fresh oregano and serve with grated Parmesan cheese.

Mediterranean Spaghetti

**Delicious Mediterranean vegetables, cooked
in a rich tomato sauce, make an ideal
topping for nutty wholewheat pasta.**

SERVES 4

*2 tbsp olive oil • 1 large red onion, chopped
2 garlic cloves, crushed • 1 tbsp lemon juice
4 baby aubergines (eggplant), quartered
600 ml/1 pint/2½ cups passata
2 tsp caster (superfine) sugar
2 tbsp tomato purée (paste)
425 g/14 oz can of artichoke hearts, drained and halved
125 g/4 oz/¾ cup pitted black olives
350 g/12 oz wholewheat dried spaghetti
salt and pepper • sprigs of fresh basil, to garnish
olive bread, to serve*

1 Heat 1 tablespoon of the oil in a large frying pan (skillet) and gently fry the onion, garlic, lemon juice and aubergines (eggplant) for 4–5 minutes until lightly browned.

2 Pour in the passata, season with salt and pepper and add the sugar and tomato purée (paste). Bring to the boil, reduce the heat and simmer for 20 minutes.

3 Gently stir in the artichoke halves and olives and cook for 5 minutes.

4 Meanwhile, bring a large saucepan of lightly salted water to the boil and cook the spaghetti for 7–8 minutes until just tender. Drain well, toss in the remaining olive oil and season to taste.

5 Transfer the spaghetti to a warmed serving bowl and top with the vegetable sauce. Garnish with sprigs of basil and serve with olive bread.

Three-Cheese Macaroni Bake

Based on a traditional family favourite, this pasta bake has plenty of flavour. Serve with a crisp salad for a quick, tasty supper.

SERVES 4

600 ml/ 1 pint/ 2½ cups béchamel sauce
250 g/ 8 oz/ 2 cups macaroni • 1 egg, beaten
125 g/ 4 oz/ 1¾ cups mature (sharp) Cheddar, grated
1 tbsp wholegrain mustard
2 tbsp chopped fresh chives
4 tomatoes, sliced
125 g/ 4 oz/ 1¾ cups Red Leicester (brick) cheese, grated
60 g/ 2 oz/ ¾ cup blue cheese, grated
2 tbsp sunflower seeds • salt and pepper
snipped fresh chives, to garnish

1 Make the béchamel sauce, put into a bowl and cover with cling film (plastic wrap) to prevent a skin forming. Set aside.

2 Bring a saucepan of salted water to the boil and cook the macaroni for 8–10 minutes until just tender. Drain well and place in an ovenproof dish.

3 Stir the beaten egg, Cheddar, mustard, chives and salt and pepper to taste into the béchamel sauce and spoon over the macaroni, making sure it is well covered. Top with a layer of sliced tomatoes.

4 Sprinkle over the Red Leicester (brick) and blue cheeses, and sunflower seeds. Place on a baking sheet (cookie sheet) and bake in a preheated oven, 190°C/ 375°F/Gas Mark 5, for 25–30 minutes until bubbling and golden. Garnish with chives and serve hot.

Mushroom & Nut Crumble

A tasty dish that is ideal for a warming family supper. The crunchy topping is flavoured with three different types of nuts.

SERVES 4

350 g/12 oz open-cup mushrooms, sliced
350 g/12 oz chestnut mushrooms, sliced
400 ml/14 fl oz/1¾ cups Vegetable Stock (page 34)
60 g/2 oz/4 tbsp butter or margarine
1 large onion, chopped finely • 1 garlic clove, crushed
60 g/2 oz/½ cup plain (all-purpose) flour
4 tbsp double (heavy) cream
2 tbsp chopped fresh parsley
salt and pepper • fresh herbs, to garnish

Crumble topping:
90 g/3 oz/¾ cup medium oatmeal
90 g/3 oz/¾ cup wholemeal (whole wheat) flour
1 tsp dried thyme • 30 g/1 oz/¼ cup ground almonds
30 g/1 oz/¼ cup finely chopped walnuts
60 g/2 oz/½ cup finely chopped unsalted shelled pistachio nuts
90 g/3 oz/⅓ cup butter or margarine, softened
1 tbsp fennel seeds

1 Put the mushrooms and stock in a large saucepan, bring to the boil, cover and simmer for 15 minutes until tender. Drain thoroughly, reserving the stock.

2 In another saucepan, melt the butter or margarine, and gently fry the onion and garlic for 2–3 minutes until just softened but not browned. Stir in the flour and cook for 1 minute.

3 Remove the pan from the heat and gradually stir in the reserved mushroom stock. Return to the heat and cook, stirring, until thickened. Stir in the mushrooms, salt and pepper to taste, cream and

parsley and spoon into a shallow ovenproof dish.

4 To make the topping, mix together the oatmeal, flour, thyme, nuts and salt and pepper to taste. Using a fork, mix in the butter or margarine until the topping resembles coarse breadcrumbs.

5 Sprinkle the topping over the mushrooms, scatter over the fennel seeds and bake in a preheated oven, 190°C/375°F/Gas Mark 5, for 25–30 minutes until golden and crisp. Garnish with herbs and serve hot.

Lentil Roast

The perfect dish for Sunday lunch.

SERVES 6

15 g/½ oz/1 tbsp butter or margarine, softened
2 tbsp dried wholemeal (whole wheat) breadcrumbs
250 g/8 oz/1 cup red lentils • 1 bay leaf
250 g/8 oz/2 cups grated mature (sharp) Cheddar
1 leek, chopped finely
125 g/4 oz button mushrooms, chopped finely
90 g/3 oz/1½ cups fresh wholemeal (whole wheat)
breadcrumbs
2 tbsp chopped fresh parsley • 1 tbsp lemon juice
2 eggs, beaten lightly • salt and pepper
sprigs of flat-leaf parsley, to garnish
mixed roast vegetables, to serve

Vegetable stock
(makes 1.5 litres/2½ pints/6½ cups):
250 g/8 oz shallots • 1 large carrot, diced
1 celery stalk, chopped • ½ fennel bulb • 1 garlic clove
1 bay leaf • a few fresh parsley and tarragon sprigs
2 litres/3½ pints/9 cups water • pepper

1 To make the stock, put all the ingredients in a large saucepan and bring to the boil. Skim off surface scum and reduce to a simmer. Partially cover and cook for 45 minutes. Leave to cool. Strain the stock through a sieve (strainer) lined with clean muslin (cheesecloth) into a large jug or bowl. Discard the vegetables.

2 Base-line a 1 kg/2 lb loaf tin (pan) with baking parchment. Grease with the butter or margarine and sprinkle with the dried breadcrumbs.

3 Put the lentils, bay leaf and 500 ml/16 fl oz/ 2 cups of the stock in a saucepan. Bring to the boil, cover and simmer for 15–20

minutes until all the liquid is absorbed and the lentils have softened. Discard the bay leaf. Stir the cheese, leek, mushrooms, breadcrumbs and parsley into the lentils.

4 Bind the mixture together with the lemon juice and eggs. Season well and spoon into the prepared loaf tin (pan). Smooth the top and bake in a preheated oven, 190°C/375°F/Gas Mark 5, for 1 hour until golden.

5 Loosen the loaf with a palette knife (spatula) and turn on to a warmed serving plate. Garnish with sprigs of parsley and serve, sliced, with roast vegetables.

Mexican Chilli Corn Pie

This bake of sweetcorn and kidney beans, is topped with crispy cheese cornbread.

SERVES 4

1 tbsp corn oil • 2 garlic cloves, crushed
1 red (bell) pepper, deseeded and diced
1 green (bell) pepper, deseeded and diced
1 celery stalk, diced • 1 tsp hot chilli powder
425 g/14 oz can of chopped tomatoes
325 g/11 oz can of sweetcorn, drained
200 g/7 oz can of kidney beans, drained and rinsed
2 tbsp chopped fresh coriander (cilantro) • salt and pepper
sprigs of fresh coriander (cilantro), to garnish
tomato and avocado salad, to serve

Topping:
125 g/4 oz/²⁄₃ cup cornmeal
1 tbsp plain (all-purpose) flour • ½ tsp salt
2 tsp baking powder • 1 egg, beaten
90 ml/3½ fl oz/6 tbsp milk • 1 tbsp corn oil
125 g/4 oz/1¾ cups mature (sharp) Cheddar, grated

1 Heat the oil in a large frying pan (skillet) and gently fry the garlic, (bell) peppers and celery for 5–6 minutes until just softened.

2 Stir in the chilli powder, tomatoes, sweetcorn, beans and seasoning. Bring to the boil and simmer for 10 minutes. Stir in the coriander (cilantro) and spoon into an ovenproof dish.

3 To make the topping, mix together the cornmeal, flour, salt and baking powder. Make a well in the centre, add the egg, milk and oil and beat until a smooth batter is formed. Spoon over the (bell) pepper and sweetcorn mixture and sprinkle with the cheese. Bake in a preheated oven, 220°C/425°F/Gas Mark 7, for 25–30 minutes until golden and firm.

4 Garnish with coriander (cilantro) sprigs and serve immediately with a tomato and avocado salad.

Red Bean Stew & Dumplings

There's nothing better on a cold day than a hearty dish topped with dumplings. This recipe is quick and easy to prepare.

SERVES 4

1 tbsp vegetable oil • 1 red onion, sliced
2 celery stalks, chopped
900 ml/1½ pints/3½ cups Vegetable Stock (page 34)
250 g/8 oz carrots, diced • 250 g/8 oz potatoes, diced
250 g/8 oz courgettes (zucchini), diced
4 tomatoes, peeled and chopped
125 g/4 oz/½ cup red lentils
425 g/14 oz can of kidney beans, rinsed and drained
1 tsp paprika • salt and pepper

Dumplings:
125 g/4 oz/1 cup plain (all-purpose) flour
½ tsp salt • 2 tsp baking powder
1 tsp paprika • 1 tsp dried mixed herbs
30 g/1 oz/2 tbsp vegetable suet • 7 tbsp water
sprigs of fresh flat-leaf parsley, to garnish

1 Heat the oil in a flameproof casserole or a large saucepan and gently fry the onion and celery for 3–4 minutes until just softened. Pour in the stock and stir in the carrots and potatoes. Bring to the boil, cover and cook for 5 minutes. Stir in the courgettes (zucchini), tomatoes, lentils, kidney beans, paprika and seasoning. Bring to the boil, cover and cook for 5 minutes.

2 Meanwhile, make the dumplings. Sift the flour, salt, baking powder and paprika into a bowl. Stir in the herbs and suet. Bind together with the water to form a soft

dough. Divide into 8 and roll into balls.

3 Uncover the stew, stir, then add the dumplings, pushing them slightly into the stew. Cover and reduce the heat to a simmer. Cook for 15 minutes until the dumplings have risen and are cooked through. Garnish with sprigs of flat-leaf parsley and serve hot.

Mediterranean Vegetable Tart

This rich tomato pastry base is topped with mouthwatering vegetables and cheese.

SERVES 6

1 aubergine (eggplant), sliced • 2 tbsp salt
4 tbsp olive oil • 1 garlic clove, crushed
1 large yellow (bell) pepper, deseeded and sliced
300 ml/½ pint/1¼ cups ready-made tomato pasta sauce
125 g/4 oz/⅔ cup sun-dried tomatoes in oil,
drained and halved if necessary
175 g/6 oz Mozzarella, drained and sliced thinly

Pastry:

250 g/8 oz/2 cups plain (all-purpose) flour
pinch of celery salt • 125 g/4 oz/½ cup butter or margarine
2 tbsp tomato purée (paste) • 2–3 tbsp milk

1 To make the pastry, sift the flour and celery salt into a bowl and rub in the butter or margarine until the mixture resembles fine breadcrumbs. Mix together the tomato purée (paste) and milk and stir into the mixture to form a firm dough. Knead gently on a lightly floured surface until smooth. Wrap and chill for 30 minutes.

2 Grease a 28 cm/11 inch loose-bottomed flan tin. Roll out the pastry on a lightly floured surface and use to line the tin. Trim and prick all over with a fork. Chill for 30 minutes.

3 Bake the pastry case in a preheated oven, 200°C/400°F/Gas Mark 6, for 20–25 minutes until cooked and lightly golden. Set aside. Increase the oven temperature to 230°C/450°F/Gas Mark 8.

4 Meanwhile, layer the aubergine (eggplant) in a

dish, sprinkling with the salt. Leave for 30 minutes. Rinse and pat dry. Heat 3 tablespoons of the oil in a frying pan (skillet) and fry the garlic, aubergine (eggplant) and (bell) pepper for 5–6 minutes until just softened. Drain on paper towels.

5 Spread the pastry case with pasta sauce and arrange the vegetables, sun-dried tomatoes and Mozzarella on top. Brush with the remaining oil and bake for 5 minutes until the cheese is just melting.

Spinach Pancake Layer

Nutty-tasting buckwheat pancakes are combined with a cheesy spinach mixture and baked with a crispy topping.

SERVES 4

125 g/ 4 oz/ 1 cup buckwheat flour
1 egg, beaten • 1 tbsp walnut oil
300 ml/ ½ pint/ 1¼ cups milk • 2 tsp vegetable oil

Filling:

1 kg/ 2 lb young spinach leaves • 2 tbsp water
1 bunch spring onions (scallions), white and green parts, chopped
2 tsp walnut oil • 1 egg, beaten • 1 egg yolk
250 g/ 8 oz/ 1 cup cottage cheese • ½ tsp mutmeg, grated
30 g/ 1 oz/ ¼ cup mature (sharp) Cheddar, grated
30 g/ 1 oz/ ¼ cup walnut pieces • salt and pepper

1 Sift the flour into a bowl and add any husks that remain behind in the sieve (strainer). Make a well in the centre and add the egg and walnut oil. Gradually whisk in the milk to make a smooth batter. Leave to stand for 30 minutes.

2 To make the filling, wash the spinach and pack into a saucepan with the water. Cover tightly and cook on a high heat for 5–6 minutes until soft. Drain well and leave to cool. Gently fry the spring onions (scallions) in the walnut oil for 2–3 minutes until just soft. Drain on paper towels. Set aside.

3 Whisk the batter. Brush a small crêpe pan with oil, heat until hot and pour in enough batter to lightly cover the base. Cook for 1–2 minutes until set, turn and cook for 1 minute until golden. Turn on to a warmed plate. Repeat to make 8–10 pancakes, layering them with baking parchment.

4 Chop the spinach and dry with paper towels. Mix

with the spring onions (scallions), beaten egg, egg yolk, cottage cheese, nutmeg and seasoning.

5 Put a pancake on to a baking sheet (cookie sheet) lined with baking parchment, top with some of the spinach mixture and continue layering in this way, finishing with a pancake. Sprinkle with Cheddar cheese and bake in a preheated oven, 190°C/375°F/Gas Mark 5, for 20–25 minutes until firm and golden. Sprinkle with the walnuts and serve hot.

Oriental-style Millet Pilau

Millet makes an interesting alternative to rice, which is the more traditional ingredient for a pilau.

SERVES 4

300 g/ 10 oz/ 1½ cups millet grains
1 tbsp vegetable oil
1 bunch spring onions (scallions), white and green parts, chopped
1 garlic clove, crushed • 1 tsp grated ginger root
1 orange (bell) pepper, deseeded and diced
600 ml/ 1 pint/ 2½ cups water • 1 orange
125 g/ 4 oz/ ²⁄₃ cup chopped pitted dates
2 tsp sesame oil • 125 g/ 4 oz/ 1 cup roasted cashew nuts
2 tbsp pumpkin seeds • salt and pepper
oriental salad vegetables, to serve

1 Place the millet in a large saucepan and put over a medium heat for 4–5 minutes to toast, shaking the pan occasionally until the grains begin to crack and pop.

2 Heat the oil in another saucepan and gently fry the spring onions (scallions), garlic, ginger and (bell) pepper for 2–3 minutes until softened but not browned. Add the millet and pour in the water.

3 Using a vegetable peeler, pare the rind from the orange and add the rind to the pan. Squeeze the juice from the orange into the pan. Season well. Bring to the boil, reduce the heat, cover and cook gently for 20 minutes until all the liquid has been absorbed. Remove from the heat, stir in the dates and sesame oil and leave to stand for 10 minutes.

4 Discard the orange rind and stir in the cashew nuts. Pile into a serving dish, sprinkle with pumpkin seeds and serve with oriental salad vegetables.

Creamy Mushroom Vol-au-Vent

A simple mixture of creamy, tender mushrooms filling a crisp, rich pastry case.

SERVES 4

500 g / 1 lb puff pastry, thawed if frozen
1 egg, beaten, for glazing

Filling:
30 g / 1 oz / 2 tbsp butter or margarine
750 g / 1½ lb mixed mushrooms such as open cup, field,
button, chestnut, shiitake, pied de mouton, sliced
6 tbsp dry white wine • 4 tbsp double (heavy) cream
2 tbsp chopped fresh chervil • salt and pepper
sprigs of fresh chervil, to garnish

1 Roll out the pastry on a lightly floured surface to a 20 cm/8 inch square. Using a sharp knife, mark a square 2.5 cm/1 inch from the pastry edge, cutting halfway through the pastry. Score the top in a diagonal pattern. Knock up the edges with a kitchen knife and put on a baking sheet (cookie sheet).

2 Brush the top with beaten egg, taking care not to let the egg run into the cut. Bake in a preheated oven, 220°C/425°F/Gas Mark 7, for 35 minutes. Cut out the central square. Discard the soft pastry inside the case, leaving the base intact. Bake the case and square for 10 minutes.

3 Meanwhile, make the filling. Melt the butter or margarine in a frying pan (skillet) and stir-fry the mushrooms over a high heat for 3 minutes. Add the wine and cook for 10 minutes, stirring occasionally, until the mushrooms have softened. Stir in the cream, chervil and seasoning. Pile into the pastry case. Top with the pastry square, garnish and serve.

Stir-Fried Winter Vegetables with Coriander (Cilantro)

Ordinary winter vegetables are given extraordinary treatment in this lively stir-fry, just the thing for perking up jaded palates.

SERVES 4

3 tbsp sesame oil • 30 g/1 oz/¼ cup blanched almonds
1 large carrot, cut into thin strips
1 large turnip, cut into thin strips
1 onion, sliced finely • 1 garlic clove, crushed
3 celery sticks, sliced finely
125 g/4 oz Brussels sprouts, trimmed and halved
125 g/4 oz cauliflower, broken into florets
125 g/4 oz/2 cups white cabbage, shredded
2 tsp sesame seeds • 1 tsp grated fresh root ginger
½ tsp medium chilli powder
1 tbsp chopped fresh coriander (cilantro)
1 tbsp light soy sauce • salt and pepper
sprigs of fresh coriander (cilantro), to garnish

1 Heat the sesame oil in a wok or large frying pan (skillet). Stir-fry the almonds until lightly browned, then remove with a slotted spoon and drain on paper towels.

2 Add all the vegetables to the wok or frying pan (skillet), except for the cabbage. Stir-fry briskly for 3–4 minutes.

3 Add the cabbage, sesame seeds, ginger, chilli powder and salt and pepper and cook, stirring, for 2 minutes.

4 Add the chopped coriander (cilantro), soy sauce and almonds to the mixture, stirring them through gently. Serve hot, garnished with sprigs of fresh coriander (cilantro).

(Bell) Peppers with Rosemary Baste

The flavour of grilled (broiled) or roasted (bell) peppers is very different from when they are eaten raw.

SERVES 4

4 tbsp olive oil
finely grated rind of 1 lemon
4 tbsp lemon juice
1 tbsp balsamic vinegar
1 tbsp crushed fresh rosemary, or 1 tsp dried rosemary
2 red (bell) peppers, halved, cored and deseeded
2 yellow (bell) peppers, halved, cored and deseeded
2 tbsp pine kernels (nuts)
salt and pepper
sprigs of fresh rosemary, to garnish

1 Mix together the olive oil, lemon rind, lemon juice, vinegar and rosemary. Season with salt and pepper.

2 Place the (bell) peppers, skin-side uppermost, on the rack of a grill (broiler) pan, lined with foil. Brush the lemon juice mixture over them.

3 Cook the (bell) peppers until the skin just begins to char, basting frequently with the lemon juice mixture. Remove from the heat, cover with foil to trap the steam and leave for 5 minutes.

4 Meanwhile, scatter the pine kernels (nuts) on to the grill (broiler) rack and toast them lightly.

5 Peel the (bell) peppers, slice them into strips and place them in a warmed serving dish. Sprinkle with the pine kernels and drizzle any remaining lemon juice mixture over them. Garnish with sprigs of fresh rosemary and serve at once.

Spicy Coconut Rice with Green Lentils

This recipe will serve 2 people as a main course or 4 as an accompaniment.

SERVES 2–4

90 g/3 oz/⅓ cup green lentils
250 g/8 oz/generous 1 cup long-grain rice
2 tbsp vegetable oil • 1 onion, sliced
2 garlic cloves, crushed • 3 curry leaves
1 stalk lemon grass, chopped (if unavailable,
use grated rind of ½ lemon)
1 green chilli, deseeded and chopped • ½ tsp cumin seeds
1½ tsp salt • 90 g/3 oz/⅓ cup creamed coconut
600 ml/1 pint/2½ cups hot water
2 tbsp chopped fresh coriander (cilantro)

To garnish:
shredded radishes • shredded cucumber

1 Wash the lentils and place in a saucepan. Cover with cold water, bring to the boil and boil rapidly for 10 minutes. Wash the rice thoroughly and drain well.

2 Heat the oil in a large saucepan with a tight-fitting lid and fry the onion for 3–4 minutes. Add the garlic, curry leaves, lemon grass, chilli, cumin seeds and salt, and stir well.

3 Drain the lentils and rinse. Add to the onion and spices with the rice and mix well. Add the creamed coconut to the hot water and stir until dissolved. Stir into the rice mixture and bring to the boil. Turn down the heat to low, put the lid on tightly and leave to cook undisturbed for 15 minutes.

4 Without removing the lid, remove the pan from the heat and leave to rest for 10

minutes to allow the rice and lentils to finish cooking in their own steam. Stir in the coriander (cilantro) and remove the curry leaves. Serve garnished with shredded radishes and cucumber.

Pesto Rice with Garlic Bread

Two types of rice are combined with the richness of fresh pesto dressing.

SERVES 4

300 g/10 oz/1½ cups mixed long-grain and wild rice
fresh basil sprigs, to garnish • tomato and orange salad, to serve

Pesto dressing:
15 g/½ oz fresh basil • 125 g/4 oz/1 cup pine kernels (nuts)
2 garlic cloves, crushed • 6 tbsp olive oil
60 g/2 oz/¾ cup freshly grated Parmesan • salt and pepper

Garlic bread:
2 small granary or wholemeal (whole wheat) French bread sticks
90 g/3 oz/½ cup butter or margarine, softened
2 garlic cloves, crushed • 1 tsp dried mixed herbs

1 Place the rice in a saucepan and cover with water. Bring to the boil and cook according to the packet instructions. Drain well and keep warm.

2 Meanwhile, make the pesto dressing. Remove the basil leaves from the stalks and finely chop the leaves. Reserve 30 g/1 oz/¼ cup of the pine kernels (nuts) and finely chop the remainder. Mix with the chopped basil and the rest of the dressing ingredients. Alternatively, put all the ingredients in a food processor and blend for a few seconds until smooth. Set aside.

3 To make the garlic bread, slice the bread at 2.5 cm/1 inch intervals, taking care not to slice all the way through. Mix the butter or margarine with the garlic, herbs and seasoning. Spread thickly between each slice.

4 Wrap the bread in foil and bake in a preheated oven, 200°C/400°F/Gas Mark 6, for 10–15 minutes.

5 To serve, toast the reserved pine kernels (nuts) under a preheated medium grill (broiler) for 2–3 minutes until golden. Toss the pesto dressing into the hot rice and transfer to a warmed serving dish. Sprinkle with toasted pine kernels (nuts) and garnish with basil sprigs. Serve with the garlic bread and a tomato and orange salad.

Green Fruit Salad with Mint & Lemon Syrup

This delightful fresh fruit salad is the perfect finale for a summer meal. It has a lovely light syrup made with fresh mint and honey.

SERVES 4

1 small Charentais or honeydew melon
2 green apples • 2 kiwi fruit
125 g/ 4 oz/ 1 cup seedless white (green) grapes
sprigs of fresh mint to decorate

Syrup:

1 lemon • 150 ml/¼ pint/²⁄₃ cup white wine
150 ml/¼ pint/²⁄₃ cup water
4 tbsp clear honey • few sprigs of fresh mint

1 To make the syrup, pare the rind from the lemon using a potato peeler.

2 Put the lemon rind into a saucepan with the wine, water and honey. Heat and simmer gently for 10 minutes. Remove from the heat. Add the sprigs of mint and leave to cool.

3 Slice the melon in half and scoop out the seeds. Use a melon baller or a teaspoon to make melon balls.

4 Core and chop the apples. Peel and slice the kiwi fruit.

5 Strain the cooled syrup into a serving bowl, removing and reserving the lemon rind and discarding the mint sprigs. Add the apple, grapes, kiwi and melon. Stir through gently to mix.

6 Serve, decorated with sprigs of fresh mint and some of the reserved lemon rind.

Blackberry, Apple & Fresh Fig Compote with Honey Yogurt

Elderflower cordial is used in the syrup for this refreshing fruit compote, giving it a delightfully summery flavour.

SERVES 4

1 lemon
60 g/2 oz/¼ cup caster (superfine) sugar
4 tbsp elderflower cordial
300 ml/½ pint/1¼ cups water
4 dessert (eating) apples
250 g/8 oz/2 cups blackberries
2 fresh figs

Honey yogurt:
150 ml/5 fl oz/⅔ cup thick, creamy natural yogurt
2 tbsp clear honey

1 Pare the rind from the lemon using a potato peeler. Squeeze the juice. Put the lemon rind and juice into a saucepan with the sugar, elderflower cordial and water. Heat gently and simmer, uncovered, for 10 minutes.

2 Peel, core and slice the apples, and add them to the saucepan. Simmer gently for 4–5 minutes until just tender. Leave to cool.

3 Transfer the apples and syrup to a serving bowl and add the blackberries. Slice the figs and add to the bowl. Toss gently to mix. Cover and chill until ready to serve.

4 Spoon the yogurt into a small serving bowl and drizzle the honey over the top. Cover and chill, then serve with the fruit salad.

Index